The Articles of Confederation

The Articles of Confederation

THE FIRST CONSTITUTION
OF THE UNITED STATES

Barbara Silberdick Feinberg

TWENTY-FIRST CENTURY BOOKS
MINNEAPOLIS

Text copyright © 2002 by Barbara Silberdick Feinberg

Cover photograph courtesy of The Historical Society of Pennsylvania (HSP), Congress Voting Independence (1904.1), Robert E. Pine/Edward Savage

Photographs courtesy of National Archives: p. 11 (#NWDNS-148-CCD-35); North Wind Picture Archives: pp. 16, 28, 51, 60, 63, 66, 69; The Granger Collection, New York: pp. 19, 21, 57; Library of Congress: p. 39; New York Public Library Picture Collection: pp. 48, 49

Twenty-First Century Books
A division of Lerner Publishing Group
241 First Avenue North
Minneapolis, MN 55401 U.S.A.

Website address: www.lernerbooks.com

Library of Congress Cataloging-in-Publication Data

Feinberg, Barbara Silberdick.
    The Articles of Confederation : the first constitution of the United States / Barbara Silberdick Feinberg.
        p.   cm.
    Includes bibliographical references and index.
    ISBN-13: 978–0–7613–2114–9 (lib. bdg. : alk. paper)
    ISBN-10: 0–7613–2114–4 (lib. bdg. : alk. paper)
    1. United States. Articles of Confederation—Juvenile literature. 2. Constitutional history—United States—Juvenile literature. [1. United States. Articles of Confederation. 2. Constitutional history—United States. 3. United States—Politics and government—1775-1783.] I. Title.
    KF4508 .F45 2002
    342.73'029—dc21   2001027441

Manufactured in the United States of America
2 3 4 5 6 7 – JR – 10 09 08 07 06 05

Contents

The Articles of Confederation

Chapter One

Uniting the States

When the Second Continental Congress met for the first time in May 1775, the main concern of the delegates was dealing with the colonies' worsening relationship with Great Britain. Ever since April 1775, when British troops attempted to seize colonial weapons and munitions stored in Concord, Massachusetts, local militia had been fighting King George III's redcoats. Yet these embattled colonists did not seek to become independent of Britain. They saw themselves as loyal British subjects, resorting to armed conflict to convince the king's ministers to restore their rights.

So far, these agents of the Crown had imposed taxes without the colonists' consent; cut off their trade with the rest of the world; denied many of them trials by jury; suspended their charters, laws, and legislatures allowing for local self-government; had their homes and businesses searched on trumped-up charges; required them to house British troops in their homes; and ordered other punitive acts.

Toward Independence and a New Government

The British government turned down colonial peace overtures. For example, on August 23, 1775, George III rejected the Olive Branch Petition. In this document, the colonists claimed that the actions of corrupt ministers, not the king, had forced them to take up arms in self-defense. They asked him to order an end to the fighting.

Instead, the king declared that the colonies were in rebellion. He insisted that they had to submit to his rule to restore peace. Not ready to submit to nor to separate from Britain, the colonists continued fighting. They still hoped that George III would repudiate, or dismiss, the ministers who were giving him such bad advice. However, the king and his ministers were in agreement about their treatment of their North American subjects.

The following year, the king further stiffened colonial resistance, lessening any chance for reconciliation. In January 1776, he hired Hessians, German mercenary soldiers, to help him keep his North American empire. By doing so, he demonstrated that he preferred force to negotiation. Also in January, Thomas Paine published *Common Sense*. This pamphlet questioned whether an island (Britain) should rule a continent (North America). Paine popularized the view that the colonies should become independent. An increasing number of Americans found that they agreed with him.

By June 7, 1776, the stage was set for Virginia delegate Richard Henry Lee to propose the following resolution to the Second Continental Congress:

Just a little more than a year after it met for the first time, the Second Continental Congress voted to declare its independence from Great Britain and to establish a confederation of states to govern.

That these United Colonies are, and of right ought to be, free and independent States, that they are absolved from all allegiance to the British Crown, and that all political connection between them and the State of Great Britain is, and ought to be, totally dissolved.

That it is expedient forthwith to take the most effectual Measures for forming foreign Alliances.

That a plan of confederation be prepared and transmitted to the respective Colonies for their consideration and approbation. [Italics added][1]

Not only was Lee urging the colonies to declare their independence, he was also claiming that the colonies needed a common government to negotiate with foreign nations and handle domestic concerns.

Although the Second Continental Congress had begun to manage and direct the Revolutionary War, it was an advisory body, not a proper legal government. Its members, delegates selected by the colonies, were expected to follow instructions from the individual colonies. The Congress met to discuss and solve their common problems. It could make recommendations but could not enforce them. At best, it was a provisional, or temporary, government; at worst, a debating society.

Lee was suggesting that a confederation be formed. (A confederation is an association of independent states. It may make recommendations to the member states but has no power over individual citizens in these states.) The colonies, on the verge of independence from the British Empire, would find a confederation more acceptable than a complete union. They were not about to exchange one form of controlling central government for another. They would welcome a confederation because it would not be much different from the workings of the now familiar Second Continental Congress. Also, the people were not yet ready to think of themselves as Americans and support a central government. Their loyalties were much more local; they were Marylanders, New Yorkers, and Pennsylvanians, for example. What's more, their studies of ancient history led them to believe that republics, countries not ruled by monarchs, were suitable only for small areas. The thirteen colonies stretched for hundreds of miles along the eastern seaboard.

These were just some of the obstacles that made it difficult to unite the states. As a result, the plan of confederation developed by the Continental Congress was piecemeal and haphazard and took several years to win acceptance by the states. Other problems arose when this first constitution, the Articles of Confederation, was put into effect. Those problems eventually proved so overwhelming that a new constitution and a different plan of government became necessary. Yet the legacy of the Articles of Confederation remains an important part of America's heritage, worth studying. After all, it was a people's first experiment in self-government in modern history. Monarchs governed the rest of the eighteenth-century world. They were watching to see whether the Americans would succeed or fail.

On June 3, 1776, days before Lee's dramatic proposal, delegate John Adams of Massachusetts had complained, "I fear we cannot proceed systematically, and that we shall be obliged to declare ourselves independent States, before we confederate, and indeed before all the colonies have established their governments."[2] He was right. Indeed, on May 10, 1776, the Continental Congress had urged the people of the colonies to form their own state governments to replace the local assemblies that had been conducting public affairs after British troops and colonists began fighting. Following Congress's recommendation, between 1776 and 1780, most of the states drafted written constitutions, defining and limiting what governments could do. Often, the legislature, or lawmaking body, made up of a single chamber or house, was the most powerful branch of state government. These state lawmakers instructed their delegates how to vote on matters before the Second Continental Congress.

Although John Adams seconded Lee's June 7 motion for independence and confederation, neither he nor any other delegate could vote on the measure right away. That decision was postponed until July. The delegates had to relay the proposal to their own governments and vote as they were told. It could take six to nine days for mail to travel between New York and Boston, a month between Georgia and New Hampshire.[3]

Also, delegates from Pennsylvania, New York, New Jersey, and Delaware did not have authorization to support independence. Their governments still hoped that reconciliation with Britain might be possible. If the vote had taken place on June 7, these states might have withdrawn from the Congress and, quite possibly, left the intended union. Delaying the decision gave the reluctant states time to adjust to the idea of separating from Britain and to issue new instructions to their delegates. Meanwhile members of the Congress prepared for the expected outcome. On June 11, they appointed a committee to compose a declaration of independence, and on June 12, they named thirteen delegates to a committee to draw up a plan of confederation.

The Galloway Plan

This was not the first attempt to unite the colonies. In 1643, New Englanders had drafted a plan for their mutual defense against invasion. By 1776, seventeen other proposals for confederation had circulated among the colonies.[4] Among them was Joseph Galloway's scheme, set within the framework of the British Empire. Presented to the First Continental Congress on September 28, 1774, his plan included a Grand Council to deal with matters involving more than one colony. The Council might also veto acts of Parliament affecting the colonies. The colonies would control their local affairs. Council members were to be elected by colonial assemblies, but the king would name a president-general who would have to approve all laws passed by the Council. This plan was set aside and then rejected a month later. Once the War for Independence began, Galloway sided with the British.

Benjamin Franklin's Plan

Pennsylvania delegate Benjamin Franklin offered his own plan to the Second Continental Congress in July 1775, called "The

*P*lans for the confederation government came from many sources. The title of Benjamin Franklin's plan, "The Articles of Confederation and Perpetual Union," would be used for the plan that was finally adopted.

Articles of Confederation and Perpetual Union." Congress adjourned twelve days later without acting on it. Nevertheless, Franklin's document contributed its name to the agreement that the states finally adopted. In 1775, the colonies were too torn between the goals of reconciliation with Britain and independence to focus on his scheme. Franklin had proposed an elected assembly to settle issues between the colonies and decide questions of trade, war, peace, and alliances. It would also regulate commerce and the settlement of western lands. There would be one delegate for every five thousand males. Men between the ages of sixteen and sixty could elect them. Each delegate would cast one vote. The colonies would raise their own taxes, but they had to contribute to the central treasury for the assembly's use. A council of twelve members of the assembly, chosen by the assembly, would exercise executive power—that is, carry out decisions. A majority of the states would approve amendments, or changes, to the charter of the confederation that had been proposed by Congress.

Other Plans

Connecticut delegate Silas Deane, possibly with help from his colleagues Roger Sherman and Eliphalet Dyer, presented his own plan, prepared in August 1775.[5] Deane recommended the creation of an elective assembly. Each colony would have a delegate for every 25,000 people. A simple majority (51 percent) could grant money and supplies for the Revolutionary War, but a majority of both colonies and delegates would be necessary to decide important issues of war and peace or matters affecting general policy. Congress could help settle disputes between the colonies only after the colonies' own efforts failed.

Neither Deane nor Franklin proposed safeguards for the colonies against abuse of power by Congress, nor did they describe in any detail the distribution of power between the two levels of government. Neither plan took up these problems, probably because each one dealt with the powers that Congress was already using. In March 1776, however, the issue was taken up in another plan, drawn up by Connecticut delegates and sometimes called the Connecticut plan. It placed limits on what Congress could do. In contrast to Franklin's scheme, Congress was not given the power to create new colonies or regulate commerce. The Congress was specifically forbidden to interfere with the colonies' right to direct their own internal affairs and raise taxes.

Dickinson's First Draft

These previous plans had circulated before the committee appointed by Congress finally met to draft the Articles of Confederation in June 1776. Pennsylvania delegate John Dickinson, a well-known writer and politician, quickly produced his own plan. All along, he had been hesitant to support independence because he was afraid that once the colonies left the British Empire, they would quarrel among themselves. To prevent this outcome, his proposal strengthened the central govern-

*S*ilas Deane of Connecticut proposed
another of the more influential plans in the
development of the Articles.

ment at the expense of the states. He gave Congress exclusive power over disputes between the states; the settlement of western lands; and decisions about war, peace, and foreign relations. The states could handle their own internal affairs and impose their own taxes, provided their laws did not interfere with the Articles. The states would run the militia (volunteer citizen soldiers), but Congress would appoint the senior officers. Congress was, however, forbidden to impose taxes. Each state would have one vote in the Congress, and all the states had to agree to any changes in the Articles. The delegates would be appointed for one-year terms. Each state was expected to contribute to the Treasury according to its population size, not counting Indians.

The Congress would appoint a Council of States, committees, and public officials to manage the business of the confederation. The council could supervise all military and naval operations when Congress was not in session. Then it would also serve as a central executive, issuing contracts, making payments, preparing matters for Congress to consider, and even calling Congress to meet when necessary.

Delays and Disagreements

The committee accepted most of Dickinson's plan and presented it to the Second Continental Congress on July 12, eight days after the Declaration of Independence had been approved by the delegates. They debated each article of the committee's draft and then ordered a printed version on August 20, 1776, to be used

IN CONGRESS. JULY 4, 1776.

The unanimous Declaration of the thirteen united States of America.

The text of the Declaration of Independence

for further discussion. Throughout the remainder of the year and part of the next year, the draft was discussed, put aside, and discussed again. Decisions on the Articles were postponed for two reasons. First, the war demanded the delegates' attention because the Continental Army was continuing to lose ground to the British. Second, the delegates were unable to resolve three outstanding issues: how the costs of the war should be distributed among the states, how votes should be counted in Congress, and who should have control over the western territories.

The delegates could not agree on whether the costs of the War for Independence and other government expenses should be allotted on the basis of a state's population or its wealth. There were divisions between small states and large states, slave-owning states and Free States. For example, Samuel Chase of Maryland wanted to limit Dickinson's proposal to white inhabitants of each state. On the other hand, John Adams and James Wilson of Pennsylvania objected that whether slave or Free, it was labor that made wealth so the total number of laborers should be counted. No compromise was yet possible.

The issue of representation in Congress also pitted the small states against the large states. The Dickinson draft had followed the practice of the First and Second Continental Congresses, allowing each state one vote. This principle of equality appealed to the small states. Preferring representation according to population, Benjamin Rush of Pennsylvania argued that voting by state would prolong differences among them, but said, "We are a new nation. . . . The more a man aims at serving America, the more he serves his Colony."[6] In reply, Stephen Hopkins of

Rhode Island insisted, "The safety of the whole depends upon the distinctions of the colonies."[7] In August, Roger Sherman of Connecticut suggested that the votes be taken both by state and by individual delegates.

The debate about giving Congress control over western lands was bitter. Rhode Island, Delaware, New Jersey, Pennsylvania, and Maryland had boundaries that had been fixed by colonial charters and were considered "landless" states. Virginia had land claims that extended all the way to the Mississippi River. Connecticut, New York, Massachusetts, North Carolina, and Georgia had charters that fixed the Pacific Ocean as their western boundary. In effect, the delegates were arguing about who would have control over sales of those profitable lands. Speculators, people who bought and sold land for profit, some with ties to the Virginia legislature, came up against their counterparts in the landless states who wanted a piece of the action. The arguments in Congress were framed in loftier terms. Virginia delegate Thomas Jefferson defended the existing land claims, while Samuel Chase of Maryland argued that "the small states have a right to happiness and security; they would have no safety if the great Colonies were not limited."[8]

During discussions in April 1777, a new delegate, Thomas Burke of North Carolina, raised another issue. He questioned the Dickinson plan because it had strengthened Congress at the expense of the states. He offered the following amendment, which passed eleven states to one: "Each State retains its sovereignty, freedom and independence, and every Power, Jurisdiction, and Right, which is not by this confederation expressly delegated to the United States, in Congress assembled."[9] Burke became the champion of limited government and the spokesman for states' rights. He did not want Congress to have power at the expense of the states and was concerned that they remain independent.

The Approval of the Articles

Decisions about the Articles had to be postponed while military matters demanded the delegates' attention. British General Sir William Howe led troops into Pennsylvania, and in September, he captured Philadelphia, where Congress had been meeting. The delegates fled to Lancaster and then to York. They were intent on completing the Articles, because they wanted to strengthen their position in dealing with foreign nations and the states. The delegates were eager to use the American victory at Saratoga on October 17, 1777, to convince the French to form an alliance with them. Also, they needed the cooperation of the states to reform the currency, which was rapidly losing value. To accomplish their goals, they needed a legal government.

The member states put aside most of the differences that divided them and quickly resolved outstanding issues. They adopted the suggestion of John Witherspoon of New Jersey for allocating contributions to the government. In the earlier debates, he had claimed that the value of land and homes was the easiest method to calculate how much each state would contribute. This solution was narrowly approved, with the four New

England states voting solidly against it. The delegates agreed to equal votes for all states, regardless of size. Finally, they rejected plans to let the Congress set boundaries for states and western lands. With those decisions in place, Congress adopted the thirteen Articles of Confederation on November 15, 1777. Henry Laurens of South Carolina, then president of the Congress, received printed copies of the document on November 28. They were sent out to the states for approval. An engrossed, or final, copy, written in large letters, was presented to Congress on June 27, 1778. Errors were found, so a corrected copy was delivered on July 9 and signed by all the delegates present.

Overall, there was little interest in the agreement among the citizens. No pamphlets were written, and the newspapers printed only some factual articles without comment or criticism. By June 1778, ten states were in the process of ratifying, or approving, the new document. New Jersey and Delaware were holdouts because they were dissatisfied with the boundary issue. New Jersey accepted the Articles in November 1778, while Delaware delayed until early 1779. Maryland was so determined to make Virginia give up its claims to western territory that the state refused to ratify the Articles of Confederation until March 1, 1781—after Virginia agreed to turn over western land claims to the new government. After much discussion and many delays, the Articles of Confederation, the first constitution of the United States, finally went into effect.

Chapter Two

America's First Constitution

The nation's first constitution, the Articles of Confederation and Perpetual Union, contained thirteen articles, or sets of binding agreements on specific topics. Overall, this written document discussed the nature of the association of states, limits on the respective powers of the states and confederation government, the structure of the confederation government, and methods of changing, or amending, the agreement. It was far from a perfect document, but as Cornelius Harnett of North Carolina stated, "It is the best Confederacy that could be formed especially when we consider the number of states, their different Interests, Customs, etc., etc."[1]

The First Three Articles

Article 1 proclaimed that the new confederation would be called the United States of America. This name was not new. It had been used before, in the Declaration of Independence. In referring to the common government of the confederation, the document often used the term "the United States in Congress assembled." (The word "congress" can be traced to the Latin word for "coming together," and first appeared in English in 1528.[2])

Article 2 guaranteed the freedom, independence, and sovereignty, or the supreme power, of each state. Each state was permitted to exercise every power, right, and jurisdiction, or area of control, not specifically granted to the United States assembled in Congress. Just like the Second Continental Congress, the new Congress could do only what the states let it do. As described and defined in other articles, that would not be very much.

In an attempt to create a strong national government, John Dickinson's first draft had curbed the power of the states to interfere with the common government and tried to prevent conflicts among them. The states would have kept their own laws and customs, as well as control over statewide and local matters, so long as these did not interfere with the operation of the Articles. In other words, the needs of the union would have had priority over those of the individual states.

During the early debates on the nature of the government in August 1776, James Wilson of Pennsylvania insisted, "As to those matters which are referred to Congress, we are not so many states, we are one large state. We lay aside our individuality whenever we come here."[3] He argued that delegates should represent the people, not the states, and act on their behalf for the com-

In the late eighteenth century, the states were mostly rural in character, and their citizens identified more closely with local customs and the laws of their individual states rather than with the concept of a centralized federal government.

mon good. On the other hand, John Witherspoon of New Jersey claimed that "every Colony is a distinct person."[4] He felt that the delegates should be chosen by and represent each state as a whole, not the people within each state. The Articles were broad enough to accept both interpretations, but the balance shifted toward states' rights, preserving the individuality and power of the states, in 1777 with approval of Thomas Burke's proposal, discussed earlier. This proposal undermined Dickinson's draft and became Article 2. It appealed to delegates from those states accustomed to ignoring requests from the Second Continental Congress.

Article 3 explained the purposes of the confederation, or league, of the thirteen states. They were joining together to secure their mutual defense against common enemies, to protect their liberties, and to improve their general well-being. The states pledged to come to each other's aid when attacked, regardless of the reason, be it religion, sovereignty, trade, or any other pretext for hostility.

States' Obligations to One Another

Article 4 focused on the states' obligations to citizens of other states and to one another. The stated purpose of this article was to promote friendships and interaction among people of different states. In fact, it was probably intended to prevent states from discriminating in favor of their own residents. Perhaps, for some, it represented the hope that people in the different states would become more aware of their common union. These provisions deliberately excluded vagabonds, paupers, and fugitives, people who lacked either financial or legal independence. According to the views of those times, such people did not have a personal material stake in the community. Since they lacked wealth or property, they were not entitled to the benefits of citizenship. Of course, state governors or state executives could demand the return of fugitives who had been found guilty of treason, felony, or other major crimes under their state's laws.

The article guaranteed citizens the freedom to travel to or from any state. In their business dealings, court cases, and personal freedoms, travelers were to be treated the same as state residents. That meant they were also subject to the same privileges, taxes, and limitations. Those limitations or taxes were not intended to apply to visitors who had brought property into the state and later took it with them when they returned to their home state. This polite language was probably intended to protect slave owners who might travel with their slaves.

The states were expected to grant "full faith and credit," or legal recognition, to each other's official records, acts, and legal decisions. This requirement can be traced to private international law, a series of rulings and judicial writings, accepted over time by courts in many different countries. In the Confederation, it was practical to have documents recording marriages, births, deaths, wills, property ownership, business dealings, and other important matters accepted across state lines. Otherwise, trade and commerce might have been stifled, and personal lives made unduly complicated.

This article was one of several last-minute additions to the plan for a confederation. On November 10, 1777, the Continental Congress had appointed Richard Law from Connecticut, Richard Henry Lee from Virginia, and James Duane from New York to a committee to report on new proposals. Guarantees of freedom of travel and equal privileges for visitors had been part of the original Dickinson draft. However, when it had been printed on August 20, 1776, the section was accidentally omitted. The committee restored it, making minor changes, and reported favorably on extradition (the return of fugitives) and "full faith and credit." By November 15, these extra proposals became Article 4 in the final version of the agreement to confederate.

In fact, the states did not always honor this article. Ten years later, during the Constitutional Convention of 1787, James Madison of Virginia openly disapproved of "Acts of Virginia and Maryland which give a preference to their own citizens in cases where the Citizens (of other states) are entitled to equality of privileges by the Articles of Confederation."[5]

Government Organization and Workings

Article 5 outlined the organization and workings of the Confederation government. The agreement provided for a unicameral (single-chamber) Congress. In May 1777, Thomas Burke had suggested a two-house legislature as a compromise between the big states' demands for representation according to population and the small states' insistence on equality for all states.

Congress did not take action on Burke's proposal. The states were each given one vote in Congress, just as they had in the Second Continental Congress. The Congress would meet on the first Monday of November.

The states had the power to decide how their delegates to the Congress would be selected. They could send from two to seven delegates to serve for one-year terms and could replace any or all of them during that year. They were required to pay their salaries and expenses. This would probably ensure that delegates voted according to state instructions rather than their own personal preferences or the wishes of special interests. To further guarantee their loyalty, delegates were forbidden to accept any other paid position in the United States while serving in Congress. States were often slow to pay them. In 1785, Rhode Islander William Ellery wrote to the governor, "I am in arrears for my board, and unless I am supplied with about 100 [dollars], I shall be under the painful and disagreeable necessity of leaving New York indebted to the person with whom I have boarded."[6] (Congress had moved to New York City in 1785.)

Factions

Under Article 5, the delegates also were subject to term limits, barring them from serving in Congress for more than three years in any period of six years. The purpose of this restriction was to reduce or eliminate the rise of factions and political strife. In the early years of the republic, political divisions, such as factions, were seen as dangerous because they encouraged personal ambition, greed, and emotions at the expense of impartial judgments about public matters. Carried to an extreme, they could divide and destroy a republic. According to historian Gordon S. Wood, men in public life were expected to represent the common good, not the private, selfish, special interests associated with faction.[7]

All along, there were indeed factions in Congress, pitting delegates of big states against small ones, northern states against southern states, states with claims to western lands against landless ones. When fellow diplomats Silas Deane of Connecticut and Arthur Lee from Virginia returned from France, a major rift between them split the delegates into factions. Lee questioned items in Deane's expense account before Congress. Some delegates sided with him, and others defended Deane. Deane's supporters came from the southern and middle states, while Lee's backers came mostly from New England. The dispute dragged on and on. Deane returned to Europe in 1780 and in 1781 tried to clear his name. In 1782, matters grew worse when the British published some of his earlier letters urging Americans to reconcile with Britain. He was branded a traitor and could not return to the United States. Meanwhile, Lee was seen as quarrelsome and increasingly unstable.

Factions were so widespread that New York delegate Ephraim Paine complained in a letter written in May 1784, "Judge, then, how great was my disappointment when I found caballing, selfishness, and injustice reign. . . . The Southern nabobs behave as though they viewed themselves as a superior order of animals when compared to those of the other end of this confederacy."[8] Congress appointed a Committee on Qualifications to deal with factions by enforcing term limits. Delegates from Massachusetts and Delaware left quietly when shown that they had served too long. The delegates from Rhode Island protested and refused to resign. The Congress moved on to other pressing business.

Rights and Privileges of Delegates

Article 5 also granted the delegates freedom of speech and debate and immunity from arrest while they were serving in Congress, except for "treason, felony, or breach of the peace," all criminal offenses. These were important guarantees that lawmakers had demanded ever since the struggle between the monarch and Parliament during the English civil wars of the 1640s, when the king tried to arrest five members of Parliament who opposed him. The English Bill of Rights of 1689 secured legislators' rights. Without such protections, it would have been virtually impossible for political parties or a loyal opposition to develop. Instead, criticism of a leader or his policies might have been misinterpreted as an attempt to betray or overthrow the government, and the speakers would have been severely punished.

Powers Denied to the States

Article 6 listed all the activities denied to the states without the special permission of "the United States in Congress assembled." They were forbidden to conduct international relations (including sending or receiving ambassadors; signing foreign alliances or treaties; or accepting noble titles, jobs, gifts, or payments from foreign governments). The Congress was also barred from granting noble titles.

States could not make alliances or treaties with other states unless they received permission from Congress. The Confederation was unsuccessful in ousting the British from its Northwest forts in the territory above the Ohio River, nor could it convince Spain to allow Americans use of the Mississippi River. As a result, in the 1780s, frontiersmen opened talks with British and Spanish officials to let them use the Mississippi River and to protect them from Indian attacks after Congress had failed to help them. Individual states also ignored terms of the 1783 peace treaty ending the war with Britain that required them to pay debts they owed to British merchants and to compensate Loyalists for property the states had seized.

The states were forbidden to tax imported items if such taxes might violate American treaty arrangements with other nations. In peacetime, they could not keep their own navies except when Congress allowed them to have warships for their defense. The states were not allowed to grant letters of marque and reprisal, which would have allowed merchants to become privateers and seize the shipping of an enemy nation. They could not commission warships either. However, historian Edmund S. Morgan noted that this did not prevent the states from building their own navies.[9]

States could not take part in wars without the consent of Congress unless they were actually invaded and had to defend themselves, for example, from Indian attacks, before Congress could be notified. They could not keep men at arms either, except those needed to garrison forts as determined by

Congress. Every state, however, was expected to maintain a well-disciplined militia and sufficient supplies for its use. During a war with an enemy nation or against a state infested with pirates, they had to follow Congress's regulations and cease hostilities when Congress declared the danger to be over.

The Militia

Article 7 provided that when states raised armed forces for the defense of the country, all officers at the rank of colonel or below would be appointed by the state legislatures in a manner that the individual states chose. This provision recognized the public's attachment to local militias, made up of part-time, volunteer soldiers.

Funding the Government

Article 8 explained how government civil and military expenses would be paid. After prolonged debate, the Congress had accepted John Witherspoon's suggestion of apportioning each state's contribution to the common treasury according to the value of its lands and the improvements on those lands. Congress would from time to time arrange for the survey of such lands. The states would use the results of the survey to raise taxes to be paid to the government at a time that the government set.

Once the Revolutionary War ended in 1783, the states were unwilling to contribute money to keep the government running. They had their own debts to pay off and did not want to tax their citizens further for the benefit of a faraway Congress. As a result, the United States was unable to repay loans it had received from France. In 1785, the states refused to give Congress the power to levy a 5 percent tax on imports, foreign goods for sale in the United States. Instead Congress began selling western lands it controlled in order to meet its obligations.

Powers of Congress

Article 9 described the limited powers the states allowed to the United States government, as represented by the Congress. The government alone could declare war or peace, send and receive ambassadors, and form alliances and negotiate treaties. However, no commercial treaty was to prevent state lawmakers from applying the same taxes to foreigners that their own citizens paid or from banning the export or import of certain goods. Congress could establish rules for deciding how captured ships or materials taken in combat by American armed or naval forces would be distributed. It could grant letters of marque and reprisal.

Congress as a Court

Under Article 9, Congress could appoint courts for the trial of felony and piracy cases on the high seas, or establish courts for handling the final appeals in cases of captures on land and water, provided that no member of Congress serve as a judge. Congress was to serve as the court of last resort in cases concerning boundaries and jurisdictions or other matters involving two or more states. The procedure for summoning and setting up this court was very complicated and reveals how determined the states were to control the powers of the Congress.

A state could present a petition to Congress stating the facts and asking for a hearing. Congress would then notify the other state or states and assign a date for a hearing. The agents for the two or more states would appoint commissioners by joint consent to hear the case. If they could not agree, Congress would select three people from each state, forming a pool of thirty-nine people, and the disputants could eliminate the members one at a time, until only thirteen were left. Lots would be drawn from the remaining names to select from seven to nine commissioners. If a disputant failed to show up and did not offer reasons acceptable to Congress, Congress would act for it in choosing commissioners. If a state refused to submit to the authority of the court, the court could nevertheless judge the issue and transmit its decision to Congress. The commissioners would take an oath to hear the case fairly and impartially, and no state would be deprived of territory for the benefit of the United States. This method could also be used to resolve private land disputes arising from differing grants to the same territory involving two or more states.

This cumbersome procedure was actually used in 1782 to resolve differences between Pennsylvania and Connecticut over the Wyoming Valley, in what is now Pennsylvania. The commis-

The Wyoming Valley of Pennsylvania, the ownership of which was disputed in 1782. This photograph was taken in 1896.

sioners confirmed that the valley belonged to Pennsylvania, but they recognized the property rights of the settlers from Connecticut. Because some members of its legislature also had land claims to the region, Pennsylvania would not accept the decision and sent its militia to forcibly remove the Connecticut landowners. Violence erupted, but eventually Connecticut and Pennsylvania made a deal. In a complicated arrangement, Connecticut received Pennsylvania land in exchange for abandoning the Wyoming Valley settlers' claims. In 1786, Pennsylvania finally recognized the settlers' claims after its attempt to set up a county government in the valley failed.

Other Powers of Congress

In addition to its other powers, Congress had the sole and exclusive right to set the value of the national currency and that of the states, to fix a standard for weights and measurements, to regulate and manage trade with Indians not members of any states, to establish and regulate post offices, to appoint all military and naval officers except regimental officers, and to make rules for the armed services and direct their operations. The currency requirement did not prevent the states from issuing and valuing their own coinage. Rhode Island, for example, required creditors to accept its own paper money in payment of debts even though that money lost 75 percent of its value a year after it was issued.[10]

Executive Functions

In his original draft, John Dickinson had provided for a Council of State to carry on the business of government when Congress was not in session and serve as an executive. The Articles allowed for a Committee of the States instead. It would be made up of one member from each state and have the power to appoint those committees and officials needed to manage the business of the country. It was a caretaker with very little power.

The Congress could appoint as presiding officer a president who could serve for only one year out of any three. (This was not the first time the term "president" was used. It was the name given to the presiding officer of the Continental Congress in 1774.) The Congress would decide how much money the government needed and spend what was necessary. It could borrow money and transmit an accounting to the states every six months. It could raise a navy and determine the size of the army, asking each state to fulfill its quota "in proportion to the number of white inhabitants in such State." The states were to appoint regimental officers and to raise, equip, clothe, and arm the men at the expense of the United States and march them to a designated place at a time decided by Congress.

Majority Rule and Then Some

Article 9 also set voting requirements in Congress. The vote of nine states was needed for Congress to declare war, grant letters of marque and reprisal in peacetime, enter into treaties or alliances, coin and regulate the value of money, determine the funds needed for the defense and well-being of the nation, borrow money on the credit of the nation, spend money, decide how many naval ships to build and how many land and sea forces to raise, and appoint a commander in chief of the army or navy. These powers granted to Congress looked impressive, but since it was very difficult to get nine states to agree on anything, or even to attend Congress at the same time, the list was hardly worth the paper it was written on.

Only decisions to adjourn could be made by a simple majority vote. However, the Congress could not remain adjourned for more than six months. Congress was required to keep and publish a journal of its proceedings with a record of votes.

Caretaker Government

According to Article 10, a Committee of States, made up of one delegate from each state, or a group of any nine states could be entrusted with whichever powers Congress delegated to it to use when Congress was not in session. Nine states had to agree to grant the powers to the committee or group. However, Congress could not delegate any of those powers whose exercise required the consent of nine states. In effect, the Committee of States was quite powerless.

Articles 11 and 12

Article 11 allowed Canada to enter the Union on the same footing as the states but provided that no other colony could join the Confederation without the consent of nine states. Early on in the War of Independence, American attempts to detach Canada from the British Empire failed. So only the provision about admitting other colonies really mattered.

Article 12 promised that the debts, credits, and loans of the Second Continental Congress would become the obligation of the United States.

Provisions for Enforcement, Changes, and Approval

Article 13 required the states to accept the decisions of the United States in Congress assembled on all questions submitted to them by the Confederation. They were expected to obey the

Articles. However, Congress was not given any enforcement powers. The Articles were considered perpetual, meaning they were always in effect, but they could be changed, or amended, if all thirteen states in Congress agreed and their state legislatures approved. The Articles themselves were to be submitted to the state legislatures for approval. The idea that the Articles were perpetual and could be changed only by unanimous vote made the government too inflexible and unwieldy to last.

In sum, the Articles of Confederation created a government that was totally at the mercy of the states. Also, it lacked jurisdiction over the citizens within the states. The delegates began to realize that many mechanisms for effective government were missing from the Articles. They then proceeded to fill in the blanks.

Chapter Three

Filling in the Blanks

The federal government under the Articles of Confederation was weak, as its founders intended. It lacked an executive branch, a judiciary, and a permanent home, or seat of government. Also, delegate absenteeism was widespread, and those who did attend the meetings of Congress lacked the power to enforce government decisions. As a result, it was difficult for Congress to fund its expenses, manage western lands, and put down local uprisings. However, the delegates searched for ways to improve the system and make it work. To a modest degree, they succeeded.

The Committee of States as a Temporary Executive

Articles 9 and 10 laid the groundwork for an executive branch by creating a Committee of States to meet and run the government when Congress was not in session. It was used just once, in 1784. Congress had been in session steadily since 1775, and most members wanted a rest. Thomas Jefferson feared that without some symbol of the confederation government in place, the people might become accustomed to doing without one.[1] He helped push through Congress a demand that it meet. The committee assembled briefly on June 4, chose a chairman, and adjourned until June 26. However, it became increasingly difficult to raise a quorum, the minimum number of members present for business to be conducted. Delegates from New Jersey, Massachusetts, and New Hampshire simply mounted their horses and rode home. One, Francis Dana of Massachusetts, wrote, "We shall not make up a Committee of States. I am very indifferent about it, because I am satisfied the public Interests will receive no prejudice from the circumstance of their *not* meeting."[2] He perhaps voiced the sentiments of all the other absentees. The remaining delegates lingered for another ten days, hoping for a quorum, before leaving. Jefferson was disappointed by the failure of the Committee of States, but by the end of November, Congress reassembled, and the work of the government continued.

The President as Executive

The limited duties of the president of the Congress included the ceremonial tasks of a head of state. So he entertained important visitors to the United States. As the executive officer of Congress, he was expected to handle correspondence to and from state officials, the military, and American diplomats. Committees of

Congress, the secretary of the Congress, and later departments of the government helped him discharge this duty. It could be a burden because the president was also expected to serve as a delegate from his home state. In 1783, President Elias Boudinot, delegate from New Jersey, wrote, "I am heartily tired of my station and rejoice at my approach to obscurity."[3]

Executive Departments

The rise of government departments was an important step in the development of an executive branch. One government department was created even before the Confederation. This was the Post Office, directed by a postmaster general. Benjamin Franklin was at the helm until 1775, when he went to France to raise money for the rebellious colonies. His son-in-law Richard Bache took over in 1776. Ebenezer Hazard replaced Bache in 1782. By 1782, the Post Office had twenty-six riders carrying mail.[4]

Other departments came later. At first, the Congress, mindful of the unchecked power of British governors, had wanted to take on the tasks of executive departments. To that end, delegates themselves served on boards and committees dealing with finance, foreign affairs, and other matters. Finally, in 1781, overwhelmed by these duties as well as the need to represent the interests of their states, they appointed single executives in charge of the departments of war, foreign affairs, finance, and marine affairs. Alexander McDougall, the nominee for secretary of marine affairs, did not accept the post because Congress refused to let him also keep his rank in the army. Congress did not elect a replacement for him. Within a few months, naval responsibilities were assigned to the superintendent of finance. Praising the decision to have a secretary of foreign affairs, delegate John Jay from New York wrote, "One good private correspondent would be worth twenty standing committees."[5]

The War Department was headed first by General Benjamin Lincoln, then by Joseph Carleton, and finally by General Henry Knox in 1785. Among his duties, the secretary directed superintendents of Indian affairs, frontier defense, deployment of troops, and the storage of military supplies. By 1788, Knox was assisted by three clerks and a messenger.[6] Knox had performed his duties so satisfactorily that he and his department later served the new government of President George Washington.

Robert Livingston of New York was the nation's first secretary of foreign affairs. After he resigned, Boudinot, the president of Congress, assumed those responsibilities until Congress could agree on a replacement. That is why Boudinot could not wait to retire! In May 1784, John Jay took over as secretary of foreign affairs. With Congress's blessing, his office replied to and stored all letters relating to foreign relations. The staff included an undersecretary, doorkeeper, messenger, clerks, and three interpreters.[7] Jay dealt with foreign treaties, trade problems, and negotiations with other nations. He came to Congress, and unlike modern secretaries of state, who are not members of Congress, he sat on committees and took part in debates.

General Benjamin Lincoln, head of the War Department under the Articles

Robert Morris, a delegate from Pennsylvania, served as superintendent of finance from 1781 to 1784. He was the financial genius who shaped the future of the American economy. In 1781, Congress, pressed for funds, accepted his plan to set up a national bank to make short-term loans to the government and pay interest on the national debt, money that Congress had already borrowed. The bank opened for business in 1782. In 1784, Congress approved Morris's plan, with additions by Thomas Jefferson, to base the nation's coinage on the decimal system, setting the dollar at one hundred cents.

In 1784, Morris retired under fire. He had been severely criticized by members of Congress for ensuring that his business partners and associates benefited from the Confederation's dealings. For example, he saw to it that his associates John Ross, John Langdon, and Haym Solomon were paid from monies held by Dutch and French bankers, leaving little or nothing for other U.S. creditors (people to whom the Confederation owed money). This business dealing led to charges that he used his public office for private gain.

Quite the contrary was true. He even took out personal loans to help finance the government when the states delayed in contributing money for its needs. However, he did commingle his personal funds with government monies. This made it difficult to determine whether the amounts he spent belonged to him or to the government. Morris was replaced by a treasury board, three officials who were empowered to control the Confederation's finances.

A Proposal for Federal Courts

The Articles of Confederation did not provide for a federal court system. Article 9 had merely permitted the creation of some courts to hear crimes on the high seas and provided a cumbersome legal mechanism for solving state boundary problems. In 1786, a committee of Congress proposed a number of additional articles to strengthen and improve the Confederation. These reforms were largely ignored because by that time, the states were considering a more thorough overhaul of the government. The proposed Article 19 gave Congress the power to define the crimes of treason (betraying one's country) and establish a court to hear cases involving wrongdoing by any officials Congress had appointed. The court would also hear appeals from state courts in all cases dealing with the interpretation of treaties, federal regulation of trade and commerce, collection of federal revenues, and cases where the United States was a party. It contained guarantees for trial by jury and habeas corpus (a writ requiring courts to produce people in custody and explain why they are being held). Seven judges from different parts of the Union would serve on the court.

A National Capital

The Articles of Confederation failed to supply Congress with a permanent home, a seat of government or capital. Congress usually met in Philadelphia, the largest American city at that time.

During the Revolutionary War, however, to avoid capture by the British, the delegates escaped to Baltimore in 1776-1777. They sought refuge in Lancaster and York, Pennsylvania, in 1777-1778. From 1778 to 1783, they returned to Philadelphia and then abandoned the city forever as a result of a mutiny.

On June 21, 1783, four or five hundred soldiers surrounded the Philadelphia State House, where Congress was meeting. The soldiers demanded back pay and the right to choose their own officers. They threatened, "You have only twenty minutes to deliberate on this important matter."[8] The state militia of Pennsylvania sided with the mutineers, so Congress had to send a message to General Washington in New York for help. Meanwhile the soldiers forgot their twenty-minute deadline. Fired up by whiskey, they pointed their muskets at the State House windows and shouted insults at the delegates. At three o'clock, the frightened delegates filed out of the building. This was the time they usually adjourned for the day. They ignored the soldiers' jeers and insults. Within a few days, the mutiny ended. The discontented soldiers surrendered to state authorities once they learned that loyal troops were on the way to put down their rebellion.

Congress then left Philadelphia for the safety of Princeton, New Jersey. There the delegates debated an offer made earlier in the month to construct a federal district on the Potomac River near Georgetown, Maryland. (This proposal did not gain widespread acceptance until 1790.) Facilities in Princeton proved too cramped and crowded, so four months later, Congress relocated to Annapolis, Maryland, then in 1784 to Trenton, New Jersey, and in 1785 to New York City, which became its final home. These moves were one reason attendance in Congress was so poor. The delegates had to find out where they were going to meet and then travel there. With the government in town, local merchants often raised prices for lodgings and meals.

Absenteeism

There were other reasons for absenteeism as well. Delegates were reluctant to leave their businesses or lands for long periods of time, to be parted from their loved ones, and to spend so much time indoors in a distant city or town on thankless, tedious tasks. New York delegate Robert Livingston summed up their complaints: "The Legislature have again drawn me from domestick [sic] peace, to bustle in the great world. I am to have the supreme felicity of making a second sacrifice of my health, fortune, & enjoyments at Congress."[9] The delegates often found service in state and local governments more satisfying. John Dickinson, for one, attended Congress from 1774 to 1776 and again in 1779, before becoming a member of Pennsylvania's executive council. He also served as governor of Delaware in 1781 and 1783.

Absenteeism affected the government's ability to function. Ratification of the 1783 Treaty of Paris, ending the War of Independence, was repeatedly postponed because the approval of nine states was required. Delegates from nine states were seldom present at the same time. Part of the problem was the procedures outlined in the Articles. If a state sent only two delegates, and they disagreed, its vote would not be counted. If one of the delegates became ill and failed to attend the meetings, the remaining delegate could not cast the state's vote.

Confederation Secretary Charles Thomson kept detailed attendance records. From November 1784 to July 1785, for example, Congress met for a total of 169 days, but for 42 days, a quorum (the number of delegates needed to conduct business) was not obtained. Little business could be done. Finally, Congress voted to send the states monthly reports on absenteeism, but this did not help. On January 31, 1786, President David Ramsay circulated a letter to the states, informing them, "Three months of the federal year are now compleated [sic] and in that whole period no more than seven states have at any one time been represented."[10]

Among the proposals drafted by the 1786 committee of Congress to strengthen the Confederation was Article 20, requiring states to elect their delegates at a certain time and send them to Congress by the first of November, the beginning of the federal year. Any delegates who left without permission would be barred from holding federal office.[11] Like the other reform articles, this measure did not pass.

Paying for Government Expenses

Congress had difficulty raising money to pay off war debts and pay for its expenses. Under the Articles, all monies for the common government were granted by the states. During the war both the national government and the states printed their own currency. The national government printed more and more paper money, called "Continentals," to meet its bills. This inflated the currency, reducing its value so it purchased less and less. By 1781, Continentals were almost worthless and were soon abandoned. The government still needed money to pay its operating expenses, foreign loans, and war debts.

The states were reluctant to pay their fair share of government expenses—especially after the Revolution was won. Superintendent of Finance Robert Morris pointed out that between 1781 and 1784, the states had paid in only $1.486 million of the $6.523 million they owed to the government.[12] They were busy paying off their own war debts. In 1783, the states rejected a funding proposal to allow the Congress to collect an impost, or tax on imports, goods brought into the United States from abroad.

The measure was rejected because it gave the government too much power. Besides, the states profited by regulating trade themselves. Since Congress did not have the power to regulate commerce among the states, the states were collecting fees on goods brought in from other states on foreign ships. In 1783, South Carolina passed an impost law collecting fees on American goods imported to the state. In 1785, Rhode Island used protective tariffs, taxes collected on imported goods, to protect and encourage the development of American industries. In 1787, New York passed a law that required New Jersey and Connecticut

Since the states could impose whatever taxes they desired, the regulation of their own shipping concerns was more lucrative for them than regulation by Congress. This scene shows the dock of a tobacco warehouse in Virginia.

to pay it fees four times higher for foreign goods than it charged for American ones.[13] The states neither wanted nor needed the confederation government as a rival. Also, southern shippers feared that this measure would make them too dependent on northern shipping, because the tax would discourage foreign ships from entering their ports. As agricultural states they were very dependent on shipping to sell their produce.

A second funding proposal, also introduced in 1783, would have assessed the states according to the size of their populations, including three-fifths of all slaves. This plan revived old arguments. It divided the large states against the smaller ones. It also antagonized the slaveholding South. As a result, it was discarded.

Under its 1786 reform proposals, Congress wanted to add Articles 15–18 to the Confederation agreement to solve its financial problems. Article 15 arranged to charge late fees of 10 percent a year to states that failed to pay their quotas to Congress on time. Article 16 would have let Congress assess and collect taxes in states that failed to pass laws to fund the government. Article 17 provided interest payments to states that contributed more than their share and required states in arrears to pay interest. Article 18 allowed Congress to determine the money it needed for periods of up to fifteen years. If eleven states approved, then it would be binding on the rest. Although these reforms were not made, all was not lost. By 1787 the amount of debt owed by the federal government to its citizens was reduced to around $27 million, while debt owed to foreign nations was estimated at about $10 million.[14] This was an impressive achievement since educated guesses place the original total debt at as much as $400 million.[15]

Land Issues

Early in the history of the American republic, land issues had plagued the Continental Congress and even delayed the birth of the Confederation. First, Massachusetts, Virginia, Connecticut, New York, North Carolina, and Georgia had sometimes competing claims to western lands and generous, ill-defined boundaries. In the middle of a war with Great Britain, Congress did not want to have to decide among these conflicting claims. Second, the landless states, Maryland, Delaware, Pennsylvania, Rhode Island, and New Jersey, wanted Congress to occupy the western lands. They claimed that the landed states, those with ill-defined boundaries, would be able to sell off their territories and use the money to reduce the need for taxes. As a result, people would flock to these states, depopulating the states with fixed boundaries. Third, speculators from Maryland, Pennsylvania, and New Jersey, who had bought acreage in the disputed western areas, were eager to protect their own titles to the land and to limit the claims of the landed states. Arguing that Congress inherited Britain's control over unoccupied territory, they and their states urged Congress to recognize their land claims.

With victory over Britain, the states had to come to terms with the problem of the western territories. Maryland insisted on waiting until Virginia ceded its western land to the United States before it would ratify the Articles of Confederation. In doing so, Maryland isolated itself from and antagonized the other states. William Whipple, the delegate from New Hampshire, stated that Maryland "has seldom done anything with good Grace. She has been a froward hussey.[sic]"[16] However, Virginia became more willing to compromise because traders, speculators, and squatters were settling on its disputed lands. The landless states were willing to accept Virginia's conditions: (1) that the lands be held in common by the nation; (2) that the new states to be carved out

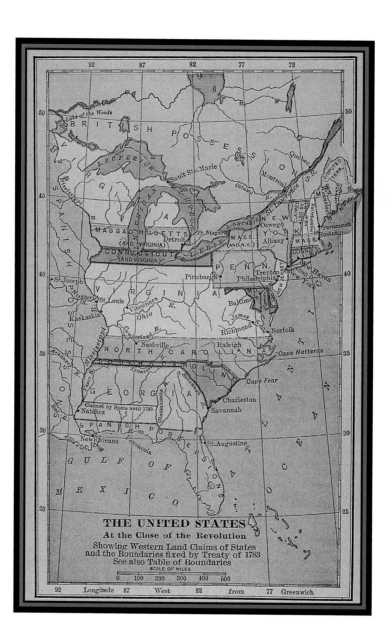

THE UNITED STATES
At the Close of the Revolution
Showing Western Land Claims of States
and the Boundaries fixed by Treaty of 1783
See also Table of Boundaries

SCALE OF MILES

0   100   200   300   400   500

of this territory be between 100 and 150 miles (259 and 389 kilometers) square; (3) that the new states be admitted to the Union on an equal footing with the existing states. Congress, not the landed states, would control the development of the West. By 1781, Maryland approved the Articles.

Approval of Virginia's land cession was held up until 1784 because the states kept arguing over the speculators' claims. The bickering among the states was so intense that James Madison commented, "The present Union will but little survive the present war."[17] The issue was resolved in 1784, because Virginia had been busy selling off land, and the delegates realized that if they did not act soon, the Confederation government would lose a major source of funding.

With the Virginia cession in mind, Congress had Thomas Jefferson prepare what became the Land Ordinance Act of 1784. It set up boundaries for future states and promised settlers that they could establish their own governments once the population reached 20,000 and be admitted to the Union on an equal basis with the thirteen original states. North Carolina had already ceded territory (which eventually became the state of Tennessee) to the Confederation. Then territorial residents declared themselves the state of Franklin. North Carolina canceled its cession. Nevertheless, leaders from the state of Franklin, who were mostly land speculators, urged Congress to admit the new state. Congress was more interested in getting North Carolina to cede the land to the Confederation once more. They chose to ignore Franklin's plea.

The Northwest Ordinance of 1787

Squatters were still pouring into the West. While Congress had arranged for land sales, it had failed to drive off the squatters so that purchasers from the East could develop the vacant land. The Northwest Ordinance of 1787 sought to solve this problem and others. Compared with the 1784 act, the number of new states to be carved from the territory was reduced from ten to between three and five. The number of inhabitants needed for statehood was raised from 20,000 to 60,000. Congress would give up its control gradually. Only when there were 5,000 free males in the territory could the population elect an assembly to assist the governor and three territorial judges. Most important for the future, slavery was banned from the territory and a system of public education was set in place. Creating strong territorial governments encouraged land purchases, systematic and gradual development of the region, and a united front against foreign nations and hostile Indians. In contrast to all the bickering about land claims, on July 13 the ordinance received a unanimous vote in Congress. This was one of the greatest achievements of the Confederation.

Shays's Rebellion

One of the greatest disappointments of the Confederation was the inability of Congress to deal with an uprising in one of the states. In August 1786, a rebellion broke out in the western part

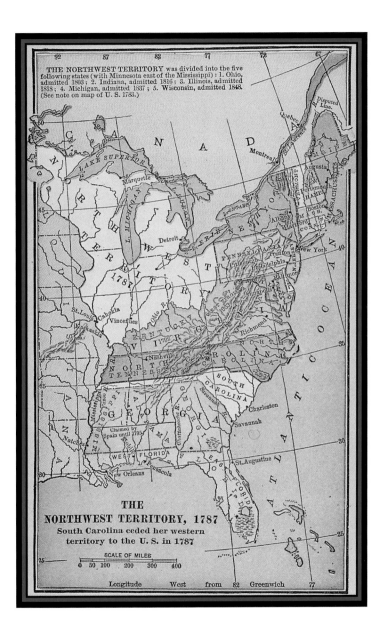

THE NORTHWEST TERRITORY was divided into the five following states (with Minnesota east of the Mississippi) : 1. Ohio, admitted 1803 ; 2. Indiana, admitted 1816 ; 3. Illinois, admitted 1818 ; 4. Michigan, admitted 1837 ; 5. Wisconsin, admitted 1848. (See note on map of U. S. 1783.)

THE
NORTHWEST TERRITORY, 1787
South Carolina ceded her western
territory to the U. S. in 1787

SCALE OF MILES
0   50 100   200   300   400

Longitude   West   from   82   Greenwich

of Massachusetts. Captain Daniel Shays, a Revolutionary War veteran, led hundreds of farmers to surround the local courthouses. Their goal was to keep the judges from deciding cases. The rebels demanded protection from creditors who were using the courts to seize their farms in payment of debts and/or back taxes. Prices for their crops had fallen so low that farmers became desperate. They could not earn enough money to pay their debts.

Congress called out militiamen to suppress the uprising, but the militiamen sympathized with the rioters and stayed home. They may also have stayed home because they did not think they would be paid for their military service. They could recall that Congress had been very slow to pay the soldiers after the Revolutionary War. In October, Congress asked the states for $530,000 to fund 1,340 militiamen to put down the rebellion.[18] Not enough money came in to pay for these troops. Only Virginia agreed to help. By the end of February 1787, the uprising was crushed by General Benjamin Lincoln at the head of 4,000 troops called up by Massachusetts Governor James Bowdoin. Shays escaped capture and was pardoned in 1788. Shays's Rebellion had demonstrated how ineffective Congress was in handling disorders within the states. It gave a sense of urgency to those who wanted to bring about much needed changes in the Articles of Confederation, and it sent them back to the drawing board.

Chapter Four

Back to the Drawing Board

Long before Shays's Rebellion, the individual states were taking steps to solve some ongoing problems. In 1783, commissioners from New Jersey and Pennsylvania had agreed to common jurisdiction of the Delaware River. In 1785, representatives of Maryland and Virginia met at George Washington's home, Mount Vernon, to settle their differences over competing claims to control navigation of the Potomac River. They also decided to coordinate their currencies and customs duties. Afterward John Jay of New York could write: "We are neither so wise nor so weake [sic] as our Friends & Enemies represent us, and the fact is, that tho' much remains to be done, yet we are gradually advancing towards system and order."[1]

These conferences encouraged state legislator James Madison to ask his fellow Virginians to invite all the states to a meeting at Annapolis to discuss mutual concerns about regulating commerce. Only five commissioners appeared at the meeting in

*The violence of Shays's Rebellion made painfully clear just
how weak Congress was under the Articles of Confederation
in dealing with states' issues.*

September 1786. Since attendance was poor, they called for another meeting in Philadelphia in May 1787. While the commissioners assembled at Annapolis, Shays's Rebellion erupted.

The Confederation and the Constitutional Convention

Congress did not officially comment on the proposal for a meeting in Philadelphia until the rebellion was over. On February 21, 1787, the delegates passed a resolution stating that it would be "expedient" to have a convention "for the sole and express purpose of revising the Articles of Confederation."[2] (The word "convention" referred to special meetings designed to write basic, fundamental laws, or to approve such laws.) No doubt, the rebellion convinced even the most reluctant delegates that something had to be done. The resolution was a compromise. It gave the Confederation's blessing to the convention while trying to limit what could be accomplished. Divisions persisted in Congress and outside its chamber between those who wanted to give the national government power over the states, a plan similar to John Dickinson's first draft for the Articles, and those who did not. The former included James Wilson of Pennsylvania, Alexander Hamilton of New York, and James Madison and George Washington of Virginia. Among others who wanted to keep power in the hands of the states were Richard Henry Lee of Virginia, George Clinton of New York, and Elbridge Gerry of Massachusetts.

In May 1787, fifty-five men from twelve states assembled in Philadelphia. (Rhode Island chose not to attend.) The delegates decided to replace rather than to reform the Articles of Confederation. More than 75 percent of these delegates had served in the Congress of the Confederation. They were experienced in government and aware of the shortcomings of the Articles. From May to September, they carefully crafted a constitution, creating a new, strong national government with power over the states and individual citizens.

Meanwhile, from May 12 to July 3, Congress lacked a quorum to conduct business.[3] Many of the delegates were also serving at the convention in Philadelphia, so they came up to New York infrequently. Finally, on July 13, with representatives from seven states present, Congress passed the Northwest Ordinance. Congress also managed to arrange for the sale of western lands to the Ohio Company.

Afterward, so many delegates were absent that the remaining members of Congress had little to do. They stayed in New York, however, awaiting the Constitutional Convention's official report of its activities. Since the Congress expected to take action on that report, President Arthur St. Clair of Pennsylvania sent out a request to the states for delegates. By September 20, when the report was received, delegates from nine states were present to discuss the proposed Constitution of the United States. Their debate was not recorded.

On September 28, with eleven states present, Congress resolved unanimously to transmit the report to the state legisla-

*In this romanticized scene, George Washington addresses the
Constitutional Convention. With the adoption of the
Constitution in 1789, the era of the Confederation and the
Articles that governed it came to a close.*

tures without comment so that the states might call conventions chosen by the people to approve or disapprove the new Constitution. This decision reflected another compromise. Congress withheld any statement of approval or disapproval regarding the Constitution. Also it did not offer any suggestions to change the document. This satisfied reluctant delegates, such as Richard Henry Lee of Virginia and Melancton Smith of New York. They had wanted to add a bill of rights to the document before it was sent to the states. However, they were willing to let Congress simply send the Constitution on to the states, where such changes could be made. Supporters of the Constitution also accepted this solution. They did not want to send the document to the states with any negative votes recorded. Supporters and opponents of the new Constitution continued their debates in print by writing *The Federalist Papers* and *Letters of the Federal Farmer* and other articles and books.

Absenteeism increased again. In October, the number of states present dwindled to seven. By November, the beginning of the government year, five remained. Business was put on hold until January 1788, when enough states assembled for Congress to meet and elect their last president, Cyrus Griffin of Virginia. In March, Nathan Dane of Massachusetts described the proceedings so far: "We do little business. Indeed we have very little to do."[4] This was why some delegates wanted to adjourn, but others prevailed. They felt it was necessary to keep up the appearances of government until the new one took over and to receive reports from the states about the adoption of the Constitution.

Some days in April, the number of states present in Congress fell to four, but by May seven states were represented. However, they postponed admission of the western part of Virginia as the state of Kentucky. To keep a balance between North and South, the delegates wanted to arrange to admit Vermont to the Union at the same time. This problem was passed on to the new government.

Winding Down

On July 11, 1788, delegates from all thirteen states attended Congress. The last time that had happened was in April 1777![5] The states were present because they wanted to have a say in how the new government was organized. They had to sort through the sudden increase in war claims coming in for settlement now that Congress was about to go out of business. They also had to deal with the western territories, issuing orders to governors and maintaining policies relating to Native Americans. Most of all, Congress had to plan for its own ending. Once nine states ratified the document, the Constitution could go into effect.

On July 2, Congress appointed a committee to advise on the transition. Their report on the dates for voting and for installation of the new government was approved on July 8. The states disagreed about the seat of the government and decided that it would stay in New York for the time being. After the delegates took up the government's financial needs for the coming year and decided on quotas for each state, absenteeism began to increase again.

October 10 was the last time Congress had a quorum of delegates.[6] Congress suffered another indignity as well. The City of New York decided to remodel City Hall in honor of the new government. The noise from the construction led the delegates to move to Secretary of State John Jay's rooms. Congress received reports on the operation of the treasury and the war departments and began a survey of the post office. Congress considered two measures: one issuing instructions to commissioners for settling accounts between the United States and the individual states; the other, ordering the secretary of war to stop giving away land to Revolutionary War officers who failed to account for the monies given them as paymasters for their troops. These may have been its last two official acts, but the records of Congress do not indicate whether or not they were passed.

The Last Days of the Confederation

On the first Monday in November, the start of the federal year, only two delegates came to Congress. Secretary of the Congress Charles Thomson continued to record attendance. From February 20 to March 1, 1789, no delegate was marked present in his records. On March 2, the secretary dragged one delegate, Philip Pell of New York, to his office and noted his attendance in the records. Soon there was nothing left for the secretary to do. On July 23, 1789, he resigned, and on July 25, he followed President Washington's orders to hand over his books, papers, records, and the Great Seal to a deputy secretary of the new

Congress. Government under the Articles of Confederation was finally over.

The Legacy

The Articles of Confederation passed from history, but its contributions to the Constitution and the new national government endured. The first five presidents and four of the first five vice presidents had been delegates to Congress under the Articles. According to historian Lynn Montross, 76 U.S. senators and representatives, 8 members of the cabinet, 8 diplomats, 29 federal judges, 46 governors, 64 state judges, and 159 state legislators had served there as well.[7] The newly established government and the states could draw upon their experience.

Under the Confederation, Americans first experimented with a national bank and coinage, with term limits for members of the government, and with executive departments. The Northwest Ordinance became an important standard for western settlements and the admission of new states. The idea of moving the seat of the government to a site near the Potomac River (where Washington, D.C., is now located) was first debated in the confederation Congress.

Some precedents set in the Articles were carried over into the Constitution itself. The requirements that states grant one another extradition of fugitives, full faith and credit, and equal privileges and immunities were reproduced in the newer document. The Constitution also contained the same guarantees of immunity and protection for lawmakers so that they could speak freely and travel to and from Congress without fear of arrest.

Regrettably, the Constitution also incorporated some negative features of government under the Articles. It protected slavery, counting five black people for every three white people, a calculation originating in the confederation Congress. It also took no steps to encourage women to participate in government. (Most states barred them from voting or running for office.) In the nineteenth and twentieth centuries, these injustices were finally remedied.

The Confederation also gave Americans a tradition of states' rights. Some states persisted in believing that they created the government and that they could withdraw from it. It took the Civil War in the 1860s to end such secessionist claims. The Constitution created a federal government of states and gave the national government's laws supremacy over acts of the states. It was formed by "We the People," not "We the States." After the Civil War, states' rights still persisted in the form of arguments to return government functions to the states and to reduce the size, spending, and power of the national government.

The Articles of Confederation left an important legacy of limited government under law. In an age of autocratic monarchs who often ruled without regard for the rights or wishes of their subjects, the Confederation showed that ordinary citizens, acting through their states, could govern themselves. They could make up a set of rules, obey them, and even discard them for new rules in an orderly fashion. That was quite an achievement!

The Articles of Confederation and Perpetual Union

Between The States Of

New Hampshire, Massachusetts-bay, Rhode Island and
Providence Plantations, Connecticut, New York, New Jersey,
Pennsylvania, Delaware, Maryland, Virginia, North Carolina,
South Carolina and Georgia.

Article I. The Stile of this Confederacy shall be "The
United States of America".

Article II. Each state retains its sovereignty, freedom, and
independence, and every power, jurisdiction, and right, which is
not by this Confederation expressly delegated to the United
States, in Congress assembled.

Article III. The said States hereby severally enter into a firm league of friendship with each other, for their common defense, the security of their liberties, and their mutual and general welfare, binding themselves to assist each other, against all force offered to, or attacks made upon them, or any of them, on account of religion, sovereignty, trade, or any other pretense whatever.

Article IV. The better to secure and perpetuate mutual friendship and intercourse among the people of the different States in this Union, the free inhabitants of each of these States, paupers, vagabonds, and fugitives from justice excepted, shall be entitled to all privileges and immunities of free citizens in the several States; and the people of each State shall free ingress and regress to and from any other State, and shall enjoy therein all the privileges of trade and commerce, subject to the same duties, impositions, and restrictions as the inhabitants thereof respectively, provided that such restrictions shall not extend so far as to prevent the removal of property imported into any State, to any other State, of which the owner is an inhabitant; provided also that no imposition, duties or restriction shall be laid by any State, on the property of the United States, or either of them.

If any person guilty of, or charged with, treason, felony, or other high misdemeanor in any State, shall flee from justice, and be found in any of the United States, he shall, upon demand of the Governor or executive power of the State from which he fled, be delivered up and removed to the State having jurisdiction of his offense.

Full faith and credit shall be given in each of these States to the records, acts, and judicial proceedings of the courts and magistrates of every other State.

Article V. For the most convenient management of the general interests of the United States, delegates shall be annually appointed in such manner as the legislatures of each State shall direct, to meet in Congress on the first Monday in November, in every year, with a power reserved to each State to recall its delegates, or any of them, at any time within the year, and to send others in their stead for the remainder of the year.

No State shall be represented in Congress by less than two, nor more than seven members; and no person shall be capable of being a delegate for more than three years in any term of six years; nor shall any person, being a delegate, be capable of holding any office under the United States, for which he, or another for his benefit, receives any salary, fees or emolument of any kind.

Each State shall maintain its own delegates in a meeting of the States, and while they act as members of the committee of the States.

In determining questions in the United States in Congress assembled, each State shall have one vote.

Freedom of speech and debate in Congress shall not be impeached or questioned in any court or place out of Congress, and the members of Congress shall be protected in their persons from arrests or imprisonments, during the time of their going to and from, and attendance on Congress, except for treason, felony, or breach of the peace.

Article VI. No State, without the consent of the United States in Congress assembled, shall send any embassy to, or receive any embassy from, or enter into any conference, agreement, alliance or treaty with any King, Prince or State; nor shall any person holding any office of profit or trust under the United States, or any of them, accept any present, emolument, office or title of any kind whatever from any King, Prince or foreign State; nor shall the United States in Congress assembled, or any of them, grant any title of nobility.

No two or more States shall enter into any treaty, confederation or alliance whatever between them, without the consent of the United States in Congress assembled, specifying accurately the purposes for which the same is to be entered into, and how long it shall continue.

No State shall lay any imposts or duties, which may interfere with any stipulations in treaties, entered into by the United States in Congress assembled, with any King, Prince or State, in pursuance of any treaties already proposed by Congress, to the courts of France and Spain.

No vessel of war shall be kept up in time of peace by any State, except such number only, as shall be deemed necessary by the United States in Congress assembled, for the defense of such State, or its trade; nor shall any body of forces be kept up by any State in time of peace, except such number only, as in the judgement of the United States in Congress assembled, shall be deemed requisite to garrison the forts necessary for the defense of such State; but every State shall always keep up a well-regulated and disciplined militia, sufficiently armed and accoutered, and shall provide and constantly have ready for use, in public stores, a due number of field pieces and tents, and a proper quantity of arms, ammunition and camp equipage.

No State shall engage in any war without the consent of the United States in Congress assembled, unless such State be actually invaded by enemies, or shall have received certain advice of a resolution being formed by some nation of Indians to invade such State, and the danger is so imminent as not to admit of a delay till the United States in Congress assembled can be consulted; nor shall any State grant commissions to any ships or vessels of war, nor letters of marque or reprisal, except it be after a declaration of war by the United States in Congress assembled, and then only against the Kingdom or State and the subjects thereof, against which war has been so declared, and under such regulations as shall be established by the United States in Congress assembled, unless such State be infested by pirates, in which case vessels of war may be fitted out for that occasion, and kept so long as the danger shall continue, or until the United States in Congress assembled shall determine otherwise.

Article VII. When land forces are raised by any State for the common defense, all officers of or under the rank of colonel, shall be appointed by the legislature of each State respectively, by whom such forces shall be raised, or in such manner as such State shall direct, and all vacancies shall be filled up by the State which first made the appointment.

Article VIII. All charges of war, and all other expenses that shall be incurred for the common defense or general welfare, and allowed by the United States in Congress assembled, shall be defrayed out of a common treasury, which shall be supplied by the several States in proportion to the value of all land within each State, granted or surveyed for any person, as such land and the buildings and improvements thereon shall be estimated according to such mode as the United States in Congress assembled, shall from time to time direct and appoint.

The taxes for paying that proportion shall be laid and levied by the authority and direction of the legislatures of the several States within the time agreed upon by the United States in Congress assembled.

Article IX. The United States in Congress assembled, shall have the sole and exclusive right and power of determining on peace and war, except in the cases mentioned in the sixth article—of sending and receiving ambassadors—entering into treaties and alliances, provided that no treaty of commerce shall be made whereby the legislative power of the respective States shall be restrained from imposing such imposts and duties on foreigners, as their own people are subjected to, or from prohibiting the exportation or importation of any species of goods or commodities whatsoever—of establishing rules for deciding in all cases, what captures on land or water shall be legal, and in what manner prizes taken by land or naval forces in the service of the United States shall be divided or appropriated—of granting letters of marque and reprisal in times of peace—appointing courts for the trial of piracies and felonies commited on the high seas and establishing courts for receiving and determining finally appeals in all cases of captures, provided that no member of Congress shall be appointed a judge of any of the said courts.

The United States in Congress assembled shall also be the last resort on appeal in all disputes and differences now subsisting or that hereafter may arise between two or more States concerning boundary, jurisdiction or any other causes whatever; which authority shall always be exercised in the manner following. Whenever the legislative or executive authority or lawful agent of any State in controversy with another shall present a petition to Congress stating the matter in question and praying for a hearing, notice thereof shall be given by order of Congress to the legislative or executive authority of the other State in controversy, and a day assigned for the appearance of the parties by their lawful agents, who shall then be directed to appoint by joint consent, commissioners or judges to constitute a court for hearing and determining the matter in question: but if they cannot agree,

Congress shall name three persons out of each of the United States, and from the list of such persons each party shall alternately strike out one, the petitioners beginning, until the number shall be reduced to thirteen; and from that number not less than seven, nor more than nine names as Congress shall direct, shall in the presence of Congress be drawn out by lot, and the persons whose names shall be so drawn or any five of them, shall be commissioners or judges, to hear and finally determine the controversy, so always as a major part of the judges who shall hear the cause shall agree in the determination: and if either party shall neglect to attend at the day appointed, without showing reasons, which Congress shall judge sufficient, or being present shall refuse to strike, the Congress shall proceed to nominate three persons out of each State, and the secretary of Congress shall strike in behalf of such party absent or refusing; and the judgement and sentence of the court to be appointed, in the manner before prescribed, shall be final and conclusive; and if any of the parties shall refuse to submit to the authority of such court, or to appear or defend their claim or cause, the court shall nevertheless proceed to pronounce sentence, or judgement, which shall in like manner be final and decisive, the judgement or sentence and other proceedings being in either case transmitted to Congress, and lodged among the acts of Congress for the security of the parties concerned: provided that every commissioner, before he sits in judgement, shall take an oath to be administered by one of the judges of the supreme or superior court of the State, where the cause shall be tried, 'well and truly to hear and determine the matter in question, according to the best of his judgement, without favor, affection or hope of reward': provided also, that no State shall be deprived of territory for the benefit of the United States.

All controversies concerning the private right of soil claimed under different grants of two or more States, whose jurisdictions as they may respect such lands, and the States which passed such grants are adjusted, the said grants or either of them being at the same time claimed to have originated antecedent to such settlement of jurisdiction, shall on the petition of either party to the Congress of the United States, be finally determined as near as may be in the same manner as is before prescribed for deciding disputes respecting territorial jurisdiction between different States.

The United States in Congress assembled shall also have the sole and exclusive right and power of regulating the alloy and value of coin struck by their own authority, or by that of the respective States—fixing the standards of weights and measures throughout the United States—regulating the trade and managing all affairs with the Indians, not members of any of the States, provided that the legislative right of any State within its own limits be not infringed or violated—establishing or regulating post offices from one State to another, throughout all the United States, and exacting such postage on the papers passing through the same as may be requisite to defray the expenses of the said office—appointing all officers of the land forces, in the service of the United States, excepting regimental officers—appointing all the officers of the naval forces, and commissioning all officers whatever in the service of the United States—making rules for the government and regulation of the said land and naval forces, and directing their operations.

The United States in Congress assembled shall have authority to appoint a committee, to sit in the recess of Congress, to be denominated 'A Committee of the States', and to consist of one delegate from each State; and to appoint such other committees and civil officers as may be necessary for managing the general affairs of the United States under their direction—to appoint one of their members to preside, provided that no person be allowed to serve in the office of president more than one year in any term of three years; to ascertain the necessary sums of money to be raised for the service of the United States, and to appropriate and apply the same for defraying the public expenses—to borrow money, or emit bills on the credit of the United States, transmitting every half-year to the respective States an account of the sums of money so borrowed or emitted—to build and equip a navy—to agree upon the number of land forces, and to make requisitions from each State for its quota, in proportion to the number of white inhabitants in such State; which requisition shall be binding, and thereupon the legislature of each State shall appoint the regimental officers, raise the men and cloath, arm and equip them in a solid-like manner, at the expense of the United States; and the officers and men so cloathed, armed and equipped shall march to the place appointed, and within the time agreed on by the United States in Congress assembled. But if the

United States in Congress assembled shall, on consideration of circumstances judge proper that any State should not raise men, or should raise a smaller number of men than the quota thereof, such extra number shall be raised, officered, cloathed, armed and equipped in the same manner as the quota of each State, unless the legislature of such State shall judge that such extra number cannot be safely spread out in the same, in which case they shall raise, officer, cloath, arm and equip as many of such extra number as they judge can be safely spared. And the officers and men so cloathed, armed and equipped, shall march to the place appointed, and within the time agreed on by the United States in Congress assembled.

The United States in Congress assembled shall never engage in a war, nor grant letters of marque or reprisal in time of peace, nor enter into any treaties or alliances, nor coin money, nor regulate the value thereof, nor ascertain the sums and expenses necessary for the defense and welfare of the United States, or any of them, nor emit bills, nor borrow money on the credit of the United States, nor appropriate money, nor agree upon the number of vessels of war, to be built or purchased, or the number of land or sea forces to be raised, nor appoint a commander in chief of the army or navy, unless nine States assent to the same: nor shall a question on any other point, except for adjourning from day to day be determined, unless by the votes of the majority of the United States in Congress assembled.

The Congress of the United States shall have power to adjourn to any time within the year, and to any place within the United States, so that no period of adjournment be for a longer duration than the space of six months, and shall publish the journal of their proceedings monthly, except such parts thereof relating to treaties, alliances or military operations, as in their judgement require secrecy; and the yeas and nays of the delegates of each State on any question shall be entered on the journal, when it is desired by any delegates of a State, or any of them, at his or their request shall be furnished with a transcript of the said journal, except such parts as are above excepted, to lay before the legislatures of the several States.

Article X. The Committee of the States, or any nine of them, shall be authorized to execute, in the recess of Congress, such of the powers of Congress as the United States in Congress assembled, by the consent of the nine States, shall from time to time think expedient to vest them with; provided that no power be delegated to the said Committee, for the exercise of which, by the Articles of Confederation, the voice of nine States in the Congress of the United States assembled be requisite.

Article XI. Canada acceding to this confederation, and adjoining in the measures of the United States, shall be admitted into, and entitled to all the advantages of this Union; but no other colony shall be admitted into the same, unless such admission be agreed to by nine States.

Article XII. All bills of credit emitted, monies borrowed, and debts contracted by, or under the authority of Congress, before the assembling of the United States, in pursuance of the present confederation, shall be deemed and considered as a charge against the United States, for payment and satisfaction whereof the said United States, and the public faith are hereby solemnly pleged.

Article XIII. Every State shall abide by the determination of the United States in Congress assembled, on all questions which by this confederation are submitted to them. And the Articles of this Confederation shall be inviolably observed by every State, and the Union shall be perpetual; nor shall any alteration at any time hereafter be made in any of them; unless such alteration be agreed to in a Congress of the United States, and be afterwards confirmed by the legislatures of every State.

And Whereas it hath pleased the Great Governor of the World to incline the hearts of the legislatures we respectively represent in Congress, to approve of, and to authorize us to ratify the said Articles of Confederation and perpetual Union. Know Ye that we the undersigned delegates, by virtue of the power and authority to us given for that purpose, do by these presents, in the name and in behalf of our respective constituents, fully and entirely ratify and confirm each and every of the said Articles of Confederation and perpetual Union, and all and singular the matters and things therein contained: And we do further solemnly plight and engage the faith of our respective constituents, that they shall abide by the determinations of the United States in Congress assembled, on all questions, which by the said Confederation are submitted to them. And that the Articles thereof shall be inviolably observed by the States we respectively represent, and that the Union shall be perpetual. In Witness whereof, we have hereunto set our hands in Congress.

DONE at Philadelphia, in the State of Pennsylvania, the 9th day of July, in the Year of our Lord 1778, and in the third year of the independence of America.

The aforesaid articles of confederation were finally ratified on the first day of March 1781; the state of Maryland having, by their Members in Congress, on that day acceded thereto, and completed the same.

New Hampshire:
JOSIAH BARTLETT
JOHN WENTWORTH, jun.

Massachusetts Bay:
JOHN HANCOCK
SAMUEL ADAMS
ELBRIDGE GERRY
FRANCIS DANA
JAMES LOVELL
SAMUEL HOLTEN

Rhode Island and Providence Plantations:
WILLIAM ELLERY
HENRY MARCHANT
JOHN COLLINS

Connecticut:
ROGER SHERMAN
SAMUEL HUNTINGTON
OLIVER WOLCOTT
TITUS HOSMER
ANDREW ADAMS

New York:
JAMES DUANE
FRANCIS LEWIS
WILLIAM DUER
GOUVERNEUR MORRIS

New Jersey:
JOHN WITHERSPOON
NATHANIEL SCUDDER

Pennsylvania:
ROBERT MORRIS
DANIEL ROBERDEAU
JOHN BAYARD SMITH
WILLIAM CLINGAN
JOSEPH REED

Delaware:
THOMAS M'KEAN
JOHN DICKINSON
NICHOLAS VAN DYKE

Maryland:
JOHN HANSON
DANIEL CARROLL

Virginia:
RICHARD HENRY LEE
JOHN BANISTER
THOMAS ADAMS
JOHN HARVIE
FRANCIS LIGHTFOOT LEE

N. Carolina:
JOHN PENN
CORNELIUS HARNETT
JOHN WILLIAMS

S. Carolina:
HENRY LAURENS
WILL HENRY DRAYTON
JOHN MATHEWS
RICHARD HUTSON
THOMAS HEYWARD, jun.

Georgia:
JOHN WALTON
EDWARD TELFAIR
EDWARD LONGWORTHY

Appearing in a book entitled
The Constitutions of the Several Independent States of America,
printed in London, 1783.

Time Line

1774

September 28   Jospeph Galloway's plan for uniting the colonies is presented to the First Continental Congress.

1775

April 19   Colonists resist British troops attempting to seize colonial arms and munitions stored in Concord, Massachusetts.

May 10   Second Continental Congress meets for the first time.

July   Benjamin Franklin offers his plan "The Articles of Confederation and Perpetual Union" to the Second Continental Congress.

July 6   Congress adopts the Olive Branch Petition.

August   Silas Deane's plan of confederation is presented.

August 23   King George III responds to the petition by declaring the colonies in rebellion.

September 25	American forces invade Canada and in December are forced to retreat.

1776

January	King George III hires German mercenary troops to fight in North America.
January 10	Thomas Paine publishes *Common Sense*.
May 10	Congress urges the people of the colonies to form their own state governments.
June 7	Virginia delegate Richard Henry Lee proposes that the colonies declare their independence and unite.
June 12	Committee appointed, headed by John Dickinson, to plan for a confederation.
July 4	Declaration of Independence approved by delegates.
July 12	Articles of Confederation debated.
September 20	Benjamin Franklin and Silas Deane sent to France as diplomats; General Washington crosses the Delaware River with General Lord Howe in pursuit.
December 26	Washington defeats Howe at Trenton.

1777

April 21	Thomas Burke offers states' rights proposal for the Articles of Confederation.
June	Ten states in the process of ratifying the Articles of Confederation.

September 11	Washington is defeated at the Battle of Brandywine.
September 26	The British capture Philadelphia.
September 19–30	Congress flees to Lancaster, then York.
October 17	Americans win the Battle of Saratoga.
November 15	Congress accepts the Articles of Confederation.

1781 Congress creates executive departments: Foreign Affairs, Finance, War, and Marine.

February 27	Maryland ratifies the Articles of Confederation.
October 18	The British surrender at Yorktown.

1782 The first National Bank of the United States opens for business; a court set up by Congress awards the Wyoming Valley to Pennsylvania.

1783

June 21	Mutinous soldiers hold Congress hostage in the Philadelphia State House; Congress moves to Princeton, New Jersey, then to Annapolis, Maryland.
September 23	Treaty of Paris ends war with Britain.

1784	The Committee of States of the Confederation meets; Congress moves to Trenton, New Jersey; Land Ordinance Act is adopted by Congress.
1785 March 25	Congress moves to New York City. Mount Vernon conference is held to settle competing claims to control navigation of the Potomac River.
1786 August September 11	Shays's Rebellion erupts in Massachusetts. Annapolis Convention meets.
1787 May 25– September 17 July 13	The Constitutional Convention meets. The Northwest Ordinance is passed by Congress.
1788 July 25	The Secretary of the Confederation Congress turns in all official records, ending the Confederation.

Glossary

Articles Sets of legally binding agreements on specific topics.

Confederation An association of independent states. It may make recommendations to the member states but has no power over individual citizens in these states.

Conventions Special meetings designed to write basic, or fundamental, laws or to approve such laws.

Engrossed copy A final copy of a legal document such as a charter or a law.

Extradition The return of fugitives, escaped prisoners.

Executive departments Divisions of government charged with such responsibilities as foreign affairs or paying government expenses.

Factions Divisions within an organization based on differences in political opinions or support for rival political personalities.

Full faith and credit States' legal recognition of one another's official records, acts, and legal decisions.

Habeas corpus A legal writ requiring courts to produce people in custody and explain why they are being held.

Imports Goods for sale that were brought in from a foreign nation.

Impost A tax on imports.

Letters of marque and reprisal Allowing private merchant ships to attack enemy vessels.

Militia Volunteer troops organized and trained by the states.

National debt Money the government has borrowed to pay its expenses.

Protective tariffs Taxes collected on imported goods for sale in the United States that are intended to protect and encourage the development of American industries.

Quorum The minimum number of people required to be present so that official business can be conducted.

Ratify To approve, usually by vote.

Seat of the government A nation's capital, where its government meets.

Sovereignty Supreme power.

Speculators People who buy and sell land for profit.

States' rights Demands to keep government functions with the states and to limit the size, spending, and power of the national government.

Term limits Restrictions on the number of years a government official can serve in office or the number of times that person may be elected to the same office.

Treason The crime of betraying one's country.

Unicameral A single chamber—as in a legislature or lawmaking body.

Source Notes

Chapter One

1. Pauline Maier, *American Scripture: Making the Declaration of Independence* (New York: Vintage Books, 1998), p. 41.
2. Jack N. Rakove, *The Beginnings of National Politics* (Baltimore: Johns Hopkins University Press, 1982), p. 98.
3. Lynn Montross, *The Reluctant Rebels* (New York: Harper & Brothers, 1950), p. 26.
4. Montross, p. 172.
5. Rakove, footnote, p. 138.
6. Edmund Cody Burnett, *The Continental Congress* (New York: W.W. Norton, 1964), p. 224.
7. Burnett.
8. Burnett, p. 223.
9. Gordon S. Wood, *The Creation of the American Republic 1776-1787* (New York: W.W. Norton, 1993), p. 358.

Chapter Two

1. Edmund Cody Burnett, *The Continental Congress* (New York: W.W. Norton, 1964), p. 255.

2. Paul Dickson and Paul Clancy, *The Congress Dictionary* (New York: John Wiley & Sons, 1993), p. 67.

3. Merrill Jensen, *The Articles of Confederation* (Madison: University of Wisconsin Press, 1970), p. 168.

4. Jensen, p. 169.

5. *The Records of the Federal Convention of 1787*, ed. Max Farrand, 4 vols. (New Haven: Yale University Press, 1966) I, 317.

6. Lynn Montross, *The Reluctant Rebels* (New York: Harper & Brothers, 1950), p. 383.

7. Gordon S. Wood, *The Creation of the American Republic 1776-1787* (New York: W.W. Norton, 1993), p. 59.

8. Montross, p. 367.

9. Edmund S. Morgan, *The Birth of the Republic 1763–89*, 3rd ed. (Chicago: University of Chicago Press, 1992), p. 125.

10. Robert A. Becker, "Currency, Taxation, and Finance 1775-1787," *The Blackwell Encyclopedia of the American Revolution*, eds. Jack P. Greene and J. R. Pole (Oxford: Blackwell Publishers, 1994), p. 372.

Chapter Three

1. Edmund Cody Burnett, *The Continental Congress* (New York: W.W. Norton, 1964), p. 607.

2.   Lynn Montross, *The Reluctant Rebels* (New York: Harper & Brothers, 1950), p. 369.

3.   Jennings B. Sanders, *The Presidency of the Continental Congress 1774–1789,* 2nd ed. rev. (Gloucester, MA: Peter Smith, 1971), p. 36.

4.   Merrill Jensen, *The New Nation* (Boston: Northeastern University Press, 1981), p. 363.

5.   Burnett, p. 490.

6.   Jensen, p. 365

7.   Jensen, p. 365.

8.   Burnett, p. 577 or Montross, p. 351.

9.   Jack N. Rakove, *The Beginnings of National Politics* (Baltimore: Johns Hopkins University Press, 1982), p. 233.

10.   Montross, p. 383.

11.   Jensen, p. 420.

12.   Montross, p. 362.

13.   Jensen, p. 339.

14.   Robert A. Becker, "Currency, Taxation, and Finance 1775-1787," *The Blackwell Encyclopedia of the American Revolution,* eds. Jack P. Greene and J. R. Pole (Oxford: Blackwell Publishers, 1994), p. 372.

15.   Jensen, p. 382.

16.   Robert W. Hoffert, *A Politics of Tensions* (Niwot, CO: University of Colorado Press, 1992), p. 92.

17.   Peter S. Onuf, "The West: Territory, States, and Confederation," *The Blackwell Encyclopedia of the American Revolution*, p. 346.

18. E. Wayne Carp, "Demobilization and National Defense," *The Blackwell Encyclopedia of the American Revolution*, p. 359.

Chapter Four

1. Jack Rakove, *The Beginnings of National Politics* (Baltimore: Johns Hopkins University Press, 1982), p. 366.

2. Mark D. Kaplanoff, "Confederation: Movement for a Stronger Union," *The Blackwell Encyclopedia of the American Revolution*, eds. Jack P. Greene and J. R. Pole (Oxford: Blackwell Publishers, 1994), p. 454.

3. Edmund Cody Burnett, *The Continental Congress* (New York: W.W. Norton, 1964), p. 681.

4. Lynn Montross, *The Reluctant Rebels* (New York: Harper & Brothers, 1950), p. 412.

5. Burnett, p. 711.

6. Burnett, p. 722.

7. Montross, p. 422.

Bibliography

Boatner, Mark M. III, ed. *Encyclopedia of the American Revolution*, 3rd ed. Mechanicsburg, PA: Stackpole Books, 1994.

Boorstin, Daniel J. *The Americans: The National Experience*. New York: Vintage Books, 1965.

Burnett, Edmund Cody. *The Continental Congress: A Definitive History of the Continental Congress from Its Inception in 1774 to March, 1789*. New York: W. W. Norton, 1964.

Dickson, Paul, and Paul Clancy. *The Congress Dictionary*. New York: John Wiley & Sons, 1993.

Greene, Jack P., and J. R. Pole, eds. *The Blackwell Encyclopedia of the American Revolution*. Oxford: Blackwell Publishers, 1994.

Hoffert, Robert. *A Politics of Tensions: The Articles of Confederation and American Political Ideas*. Niwot, CO: University of Colorado Press, 1992.

Maier, Pauline. *American Scripture: Making the Declaration of Independence*. New York: Vintage Books, 1998.

Jensen, Merrill. *The Articles of Confederation: An Interpretation of the Socio-Constitutional History of the American Revolution 1774–1781*. Madison: University of Wisconsin Press, 1976.

____. *The New Nation: A History of the United States During the Confederation 1781–1789*. Boston: Northeastern University Press, 1981.

Montross, Lynn. *The Reluctant Rebels: The Story of the Continental Congress 1774–1789*. New York: Harper & Brothers, 1950.

Morgan, Edmund S. *The Birth of the Republic 1763–89*, 3rd ed. Chicago: University of Chicago Press, 1992.

Rakove, Jack. *The Beginnings of National Politics: An Interpretive History of the Continental Congress*. Baltimore: Johns Hopkins University Press, 1979.

Records of the Federal Convention of 1787. Ed. Max Farrand. 4 vols. New Haven: Yale University Press, 1966.

Sanders, Jennings B. *The Presidency of the Continental Congress 1774–89: A Study in American Institutional History*. Gloucester, MA: Peter Smith, 1971.

Wood, Gordon S. *The Creation of the American Republic 1776–1787*. New York: W. W. Norton, 1993.

____. *The Radicalism of the American Revolution*. New York: Vintage Books, 1991.

Index

About the Author

Barbara Silberdick Feinberg graduated with honors from Wellesley College where she was elected to Phi Beta Kappa. She holds a Ph.D. in political science from Yale University. Mrs. Feinberg lives in New York City with her Yorkshire terrier, Holly. Among her hobbies are growing African violets, collecting autographs of historical personalities, listening to the popular music of the 1920s, '30s and '40s, knitting and crocheting, and working out in exercise classes.